SACRED REPATTERNING

A 90-Day Journey of Elemental Habit
Work and Spiritual Alignment

Volume II of the Holy Habits
Devotional Series

Angelyna Hawbecker

Sacred Ember Press

Published by Sacred Ember Press
ISBN: 979-8-9999040-2-7

For the people we used to be —
Tired, tangled, and still rising.
You broke patterns the world said were unbreakable.

You found holiness in healing.
This is for every tender step you took
When no one else could see the path but your soul.

CONTENTS

INTRODUCTION

Our souls were not designed for endless urgency. They were made for rhythm—cycles of expansion, release, quiet, and growth. Sacred Repatterning is an invitation to return to that rhythm.

This is the second part of The Sacred Year journey, following the tender unlearning of Shadow to Sacred. Where Volume I asked you to shed old patterns, this volume helps you build new ones—habits rooted in presence, devotion, and trust.

The elements are your teachers now:

Fire ignites courage and momentum.
Earth grounds you in safety and stability.
Air clears the mind and frees the voice.
Water softens and heals emotional currents.

Spirit holds it all, reminding you that you are never separate from the sacred. The lunar cycle moves with you, too—new beginnings under the New Moon, steady growth in the Waxing Moon, release under the Waning, and quiet listening in the Dark Moon.

This is not about rushing to a "better" version of yourself. It is about remembering that you are already whole—and choosing, one small act at a time, to live from that truth. Take your time. Let this book meet you where you are. Some days will feel like firelight; others will feel like soft soil or deep waters. Trust every rhythm, even the pauses.

You are not starting over. You are becoming rooted, radiant, and true.

WEEK 1: THE SACRED SPARK

"And then the day came, when the risk to remain tight in a bud
was more painful than the risk it took to blossom."
— Anaïs Nin

Fire is the element of ignition, of courage, of daring to take the
first step even when the path ahead feels uncertain.
Under the New Moon, Fire whispers: it is time to kindle. The
energy is not about grand leaps or reckless movement — it is
about honoring the small flame that has already begun to burn
inside you.

Perhaps you have been waiting for the perfect moment or
telling yourself you need to be more prepared before you begin.
But beginnings are rarely tidy. Fire does not wait for
permission. It exists because it must, and in its existence,
it changes everything around it.

This week invites you to remember that the spark itself is
sacred. You are not asked to have the whole vision mapped or the
outcome guaranteed — only to honor the ember glowing within.
Each small yes is a match struck in the dark. Each step forward
builds warmth and light.

May this week remind you that you are safe to ignite, that the
fire within you is holy, and that your becoming begins the
moment you choose to say yes.

Day 1: Igniting the Spark

The Elemental Pattern:

You've been hesitating at the edge, waiting for the perfect moment to begin. Fire energy is calling now—not to rush, but to kindle. There's a sacred difference between pushing and rising. You're not being asked to leap—you're being asked to light the match.

The Sacred Shift:

Fire doesn't apologize for existing. It is necessary to clarify. It dances because it can. Your desires are not random—they are the blueprints of your becoming. When you say "yes" to the spark, you say yes to life unfolding in you.

The Ritual Repatterning:

Light a candle, speak aloud: "I give myself permission to begin."

Journal Prompt: What small fire is flickering inside me that I haven't honored?

Optional: Draw or name one thing you're ready to ignite this week—a habit, a truth, a dream.

Day 2: Sacred Desire

The Elemental Pattern:

Desire has been treated like a dangerous thing. You
were taught to temper it, hide it, diminish it. But fire
is not shameful; it is holy.

The Sacred Shift:

Your sacred spark was never meant to stay dormant. What you
long for is already a conversation between your soul
and the Divine. You are not asking for too much. You are
remembering what you're here to become.

The Ritual Repatterning:

Whisper to yourself: "My desire is sacred."

Journal Prompt: If I trusted my desire was holy, what would
I allow myself to want?

Create a short mantra you can say each morning this week.
Example: "Let the fire in me rise."

Day 3: The Inner Flame

The Elemental Pattern:

The world taught you to wait for outside validation
before feeling worthy. But your fire does not originate
in approval. It lives in your belly. In your bones.

The Sacred Shift:

When you reconnect with your inner flame, confidence
returns—not because others see you, but because you do.
It is safe to trust your heat.

The Ritual Repatterning:

Place your hands over your solar plexus and take five deep
breaths.

Journal Prompt: Where have I outsourced my confidence,
and how can I bring it back home?

Day 4: Honoring the Flicker

The Elemental Pattern:

Not every fire roars. Sometimes your flame is a flicker—
gentle, quiet, persistent. You don't need to be loud to be lit.

The Sacred Shift:

Fire teaches you to honor what burns, even when it doesn't
blaze. The flicker is sacred. It's your spirit saying: I'm still here.

The Ritual Repatterning:

Sit with a single candle or light. Breathe slowly. Just observe.

Journal Prompt: What parts of me are still glowing, even in
fatigue?

Day 5: Saying Yes

The Elemental Pattern:

The small "yes" you speak today is the foundation of
transformation. You don't have to see the whole path.
Just take the next step.

The Sacred Shift:

Fire doesn't ask for perfection. It asks for fuel. The tiniest match
can ignite a wildfire of becoming. It can be something
as simple as long forgotten dream or idea. The ember is still
glowing it just needs some air.

The Ritual Repatterning:

Declare one small action in alignment with your desire.

Journal Prompt: What is my next sacred yes?

Day 6: Releasing Resistance

The Elemental Pattern:

Fear disguises itself as resistance—procrastination, perfectionism, delay. Fire melts these defenses when you let it.

The Sacred Shift:

Resistance is not proof that you are failing. It's proof that something meaningful is stirring. Let fire burn what no longer belongs.

The Ritual Repatterning:

Write down what you're resisting and burn the paper (safely).

Journal Prompt: What would my week feel like without this weight?

Day 7: The Sacred Ember

The Elemental Pattern:

After the blaze, the ember remains. Fire teaches you to sustain—
not just start. The ember glows with memory and meaning.

The Sacred Shift:

Your devotion does not need to be flashy. Let this ember of
intention carry you forward. Think of what tools you would
keep if you were the one who had to tend the fire. You are
becoming fire-tender now.

The Ritual Repatterning:

Return to your Day 1 candle (or relight one). Sit with your
journey.

Reflect: What sacred flame did I tend this week, and how will I
carry it forward?

MY NOTES

WEEK 2: SACRED FOUNDATIONS

*"To forget how to dig the earth and to tend the soil
is to forget ourselves." — Mahatma Gandhi.*

Earth is the keeper of structure, patience, and devotion. Under the waxing moon, Earth teaches us that lasting change is built stone by stone, seed by seed. Mountains are not formed overnight, and roots do not deepen instantly.

When we step into new habits or practices, it can feel overwhelming to imagine the whole mountain ahead of us. However, Earth reminds us that the sacred is found in the single stone we place today. What matters is not the speed of building, but the steadiness of it.

This week, you are invited to honor the sacred act of consistency. Tending to one habit with devotion begins to reshape the ground beneath your life. You are not failing if it feels small. In fact, the smallness is what makes it strong.

May this week ground you in patience and remind you that every act of care is a seed placed in your soul's garden.

Day 1: Laying the First Stone

The Elemental Pattern:

Earth builds slowly, stone by stone, habit by habit. There is no rush in the way a mountain rises, no hurry in the way roots deepen. Today, you begin not by overhauling everything, but by choosing one sacred stone to place.

The Sacred Shift:

Consistency is devotion. The way you tend your days is the way you tend your soul. Even one small act of care, repeated, begins to reshape the landscape of your life.

The Ritual Repatterning:

Choose one foundational habit to tend this week (a morning breath, clearing a space, honoring your body with water or food).

Journal Prompt: If my life were a sacred garden, what single stone or seed would I place first?

Affirm: "I build my life gently, one sacred act at a time."

Day 2: Listening to the Soil

The Elemental Pattern:

The earth speaks before it grows. Farmers listen to the soil, not just the sky, before planting. You, too, are being invited to pause and listen—what does your inner ground need before you add more weight to it?

The Sacred Shift:

Not all growth comes from doing more. Sometimes the most sacred work is noticing what's already there—what's dry, what's fertile, what's ready to rest.

The Ritual Repatterning:

Sit quietly with your body, your home, or your journal.

Ask: Where do I feel solid? Where do I feel depleted?

Journal Prompt: What parts of my life are asking for nourishment instead of effort?

Optional: Place your hand on the ground, floor, or your belly and whisper: "I listen to what is ready before I plant."

Day 3: Sacred Stewardship

The Elemental Pattern:

Earth calls you into a relationship with what you already have—your body, time, resources, and environment. Stewardship is not about ownership; it's about reverence.

The Sacred Shift:

You don't need more to be worthy. You need to recognize the sacred in what's already present. Stewarding your energy, space, and finances can be a spiritual act.

The Ritual Repatterning:

Choose one area of your life to tend today: your budget, your space, your schedule, or your physical body.

Journal Prompt: Where am I being called into more mindful stewardship?

Affirm: "I am a caretaker of what I've been given."

Day 4: Creating Grounding Rituals

The Elemental Pattern:

Earth loves rhythm. Your nervous system does too. Sacred rituals don't need to be complex—they just need to be consistent.

The Sacred Shift:

You deserve rituals that restore you. Even the smallest acts, repeated with presence, become altars of healing. A ritual does not have to be a big production, it can be small and quiet. It only needs to mean something to you.

The Ritual Repatterning:

Choose a grounding ritual for morning or evening: tea, journaling, walking, or breath practice.

Journal Prompt: What rituals have helped me feel safe in the past? What would I like to begin again?

Whisper: "I return to what roots me."

Day 5: Boundaries as Blessings

The Elemental Pattern:

Earth teaches us that even the most nourishing soil needs protection. A garden thrives when it's tended—and when it has boundaries.

The Sacred Shift:

Boundaries are not barriers to love; they are portals to self-respect. Saying "no" is an act of devotion to what you truly value.

The Ritual Repatterning:

Name one energetic or emotional boundary you need right now.

Journal Prompt: Where am I giving more than I have to offer? What would it look like to honor my limits with grace?

Optional mantra: "My boundaries bless all they touch."

Day 6: Reclaim the Body

The Elemental Pattern:

Your body is your first home. It remembers every story,
every wound, and every prayer. Earth invites you to
return—to listen.

The Sacred Shift:

You are not too much. You are not broken. You are sacred
ground. Reclaiming your body is not about perfection—
it's about presence.

The Ritual Repatterning:

Rest your hands on your belly or chest and breathe slowly.

Journal Prompt: What messages has my body been trying to
send me lately? How can I listen more deeply?

Movement: Gently stretch, sway, or walk—moving with
gratitude for the body you live in.

Day 7: Becoming the Rooted Self

The Elemental Pattern:

As the moon waxes, you've been building energy. But Earth asks —can you grow and stay grounded?

The Sacred Shift:

You are allowed to rise and root. Expansion doesn't have to mean overwhelm. You can move forward while staying centered.

The Ritual Repatterning:

Light a candle and name one grounding truth that keeps you steady.

Journal Prompt: How has rooting myself helped me show up more fully this week? What am I proud of?

Optional: Write a blessing for your body, your home, or your foundation.

MY NOTES

WEEK 3: CLEAR VOICE, CLEAR TRUTH

*"The truth will set you free, but first it will shatter
the chains you built to survive." — Unknown.*

Air is the element of clarity, communication, and
illumination. Under the Full Moon, Air brings light to what has
been hidden, and the truths we've kept buried rise to
the surface. Often, the first breath of truth doesn't roar —
it whispers. And yet, even the smallest whisper of truth
has the power to set us free.

You may fear that speaking your truth will be disruptive, or that
it must be perfectly formed before it is spoken. But truth does
not need polish. It only needs courage. Even the quiet
admission — I feel this, I need this, I am this — is a sacred exhale.

This week, you are invited to breathe out what has been
silenced within you. To practice naming what is real, even
if no one else hears it but you. The act of saying it aloud
breaks the old chains of silence and begins the path toward
freedom.

May this week give you breath enough to speak your truth,
clarity enough to honor it, and courage enough to live it.

Day 1: The First Breath of Truth

The Elemental Pattern:

Air under the full moon carries illumination—what was hidden is revealed. This first breath of truth doesn't have to be loud or perfect; it just has to be real.

The Sacred Shift:

Your truth doesn't need to roar to be sacred. Even the smallest, quietest admission—I feel this, I need this, I am this—is a holy exhale. The act of naming it breaks the old chain of silence.

The Ritual Repatterning:

Place your hand over your chest. Take one deep breath and whisper a truth, even if only to yourself.

Journal Prompt: What truth have I been holding back because I thought it was too small to matter?

Optional: Light incense or open a window and imagine your breath carrying that truth into the world.

Day 2: Untangling the Old Words

The Elemental Pattern:

Air moves quickly—it carries not only your words but the echoes of others. Somewhere along the way, you may have inhaled voices that weren't your own: "You're too much," "Stay quiet," "Don't upset anyone."

The Sacred Shift:

You are not required to carry those words any longer. Clearing them is an act of reclamation. You are allowed to speak with your breath now.

The Ritual Repatterning:

Write down one phrase or belief you've carried that isn't yours. Cross it out boldly.

Journal Prompt: What do I want to say instead? What is my truth here?

Optional: Tear up or burn the old phrase as a symbolic exhale of release.

Day 3: The Courage to Inhale

The Elemental Pattern:

Before you speak outwardly, you must first breathe inwardly. Air invites you to take in life—to let courage, clarity, and possibility fill you before you release them.

The Sacred Shift:

Breathing deeply is an act of trust. It tells your body: I am safe enough to receive. I am safe enough to express.

The Ritual Repatterning:

Practice 5 rounds of this breath: Inhale for 4, hold for 4, exhale for 6.

Journal Prompt: What happens in my body when I breathe deeply into truth instead of holding my breath?

Optional: Place your hand on your throat as you breathe, imagining air clearing old blockages.

Day 4: When Silence Was Safety

The Elemental Pattern:

Sometimes, silence was survival. Air became held breath. Truth was stored in the bones instead of being spoken aloud.

The Sacred Shift:

Honoring your past silence is a form of grace. But your soul no longer needs to hide its breath. The truth can live now—not as a weapon, but as a wind of freedom.

The Ritual Repatterning:

Write a letter to your younger self who stayed silent. Let them know: "You were brave. You are safe now."

Journal Prompt: Where did I learn to hold my tongue—and what truth wants to be freed now?

Optional: Burn or bury the letter in a small act of release and honor.

Day 5: Speaking as Ceremony

The Elemental Pattern:

Words can become offerings. Every spoken truth is a spell —one
that realigns energy and reclaims power.

The Sacred Shift:

When you speak with intention, you're not just communicating
—you're creating. Ceremony begins when words are chosen with
care and courage.

The Ritual Repatterning:

Speak aloud a truth you've been holding in. Let it be
simple, even if it trembles.

Journal Prompt: What would it mean to make my voice a
sacred tool rather than a reaction?

Optional: Light incense or smudge as you speak your truth
to the space around you.

Day 6: Listening with Spirit

The Elemental Pattern:

Air doesn't only carry your voice—it also brings messages from beyond. Listening is as holy as speaking.

The Sacred Shift:

Divine guidance often comes as a whisper, not a roar. When you attune your inner ear, you hear more than sound—you hear Spirit.

The Ritual Repatterning:

Sit quietly and listen to ambient sound—wind, birds, breath. Ask: What wants to be heard?

Journal Prompt: What truth have I been resisting that's gently repeating itself?

Optional: Pull an oracle or tarot card and reflect on its message as a voice from Spirit.

Day 7: Breath of Integration

The Elemental Pattern:

The breath has been your companion through silence and song, grief and growth. Now, it brings it all together.

The Sacred Shift:

You are not broken. You are breath—constant, sacred, alive. The voice you reclaim is not separate from the soul—it is one with it.

The Ritual Repatterning:

Breathe in for 4 counts, hold for 4, release for 6. Repeat three times.

Journal Prompt: How has my relationship to voice, truth, and breath shifted this week?

Optional: Record a message to your future self, reminding you: "You are safe to speak. You are worthy of being heard."

MY NOTES

WEEK 4: THE SACRED RELEASE

"You were never meant to carry it all. Even the Earth knows when to shed its leaves." — Unknown.

Earth is known for holding — memory, roots, weight. But even the Earth must release. Trees shed their leaves, soil breaks down what no longer serves, and the waning moon teaches us the art of letting go. What has been carried too long becomes heavy, and heaviness is not holy.

So often, we believe release means failure. That letting go is giving up. But in truth, release is a sacred trust. It says: I do not have to carry what is not mine. I do not have to hold what is finished. I am allowed to put it down.

This week invites you to lay your burdens gently on the ground. To remember that what is released is not lost — it is transformed. The earth knows how to compost what you no longer need and turn it into nourishment.

May this week give you courage to release what has grown too heavy, and faith to trust the holy cycle of endings is becoming beginnings.

Day 1: The Weight We Carry

The Elemental Pattern:

Earth holds. It remembers. It keeps the imprints of everything you've ever tried to manage—every burden, expectation, belief. Under the waning moon, the Earth invites you to let go.

The Sacred Shift:

You were never meant to carry everything. Releasing doesn't mean failing—it means making space for something better aligned.

The Ritual Repatterning:

Lie on the floor and feel the support of the ground beneath you.

Journal Prompt: What have I been carrying that no longer belongs to me?

Optional: Write down one thing you are ready to release, and bury or compost it.

Day 2: Sacred Enoughness

The Elemental Pattern:

The waning moon quiets everything. It says: rest, reflect, release. And Earth reminds you: you are enough, even in your stillness.

The Sacred Shift:

Worth is not earned by output. You are not behind. You are not late. You are growing in unseen ways.

The Ritual Repatterning:

Whisper aloud: I am enough as I am.

Journal Prompt: Where do I still believe I have to prove myself?

Optional: Create a small altar with one object that symbolizes your worth.

Day 3: The Wisdom of Roots

The Elemental Pattern:

In the quiet underground, roots deepen. Growth isn't always visible—but it is always sacred.

The Sacred Shift:

What's rooted will last. You don't have to force anything right now. Choose what's essential and release the rest. It's might be time to look at what is rooted.

The Ritual Repatterning:

Visualize roots growing from your feet into the earth.

Journal Prompt: What truly sustains me? What is no longer rooted in truth?

Optional: Place a grounding object (stone, root herb, small plant) on your altar.

Day 4: Release the Role

The Elemental Pattern:

Earth carries the stories we've worn, even when they no longer fit. You've played roles—caretaker, peacemaker, perfectionist.

The Sacred Shift:

Who you are becoming doesn't need old costumes. There comes a time when we have to let the idea of the role we play go. This is not betrayal—it is sacred permission.

The Ritual Repatterning:

Mirror work: I am more than the role I was taught to play.

Journal Prompt: Which roles have I carried to survive? Which ones am I ready to release?

Optional: Write the name of one role and bury or burn it.

Day 5: The Blessing of Boundaries

The Elemental Pattern:

Earth teaches protection—stone, bark, bone, shell. You are not meant to be without boundaries.

The Sacred Shift:

Boundaries are not walls—they are altars of self-worth. Each time you say "no" to someone or something that wants to steal your energy, you say "yes" to your soul.

The Ritual Repatterning:

Speak aloud: My boundaries are sacred.

Journal Prompt: Where am I leaking energy? Where do I long for firmer ground?

Optional: Anoint your wrists or solar plexus with oil while speaking your boundary aloud.

Day 6: The Sacred Cleanse

The Elemental Pattern:

Earth and the waning moon both invite a cleansing—
of space, of story, of the clutter you no longer need.

The Sacred Shift:

Cleansing is not just about dusting shelves—it is an act of
devotion. What feeling comes to mind when you hear this
statement: I deserve clear space?

The Ritual Repatterning:

Choose one area to cleanse—let it be symbolic.

Speak: I make space for what is sacred.

Journal Prompt: How does my external space reflect my
internal state?

Day 7: Stillness is Sacred

The Elemental Pattern:

After the release and the cleansing comes the quiet. Stillness is not stagnation—it is sacred preparation.

The Sacred Shift:

You've done sacred work. Let yourself receive the peace that comes after the surrender. There comes a time that we must make peace with the silence; to allow ourselves to be ok with our own thoughts.

The Ritual Repatterning:

Sit or lie in silence, hand on heart.

Journal Prompt: What am I learning to release with more grace?

Optional mantra: I am not empty—I am open.

MY NOTES

WEEK 5: SACRED WORTHINESS
IN THE VOID

"The wound is the place where the Light enters you." — Rumi.

The Dark Moon is the womb of becoming. Spirit moves in mystery — in the unseen places, in the pause, in the silence that feels like emptiness. But the void is not barren. It is soil. It is sacred potential waiting to take form.

In a world that glorifies constant movement, it can feel frightening to rest in the dark. To be still. To allow mystery. But your worth is not tied to productivity. The pause is holy. The dark is not your enemy. It is your teacher.

This week, you are invited to rest in the sacred void. To trust what is being formed beyond your sight. To remember that even when you cannot see progress, Spirit is at work. The hidden places are where the deepest roots are formed.

May this week remind you that you are worthy in stillness, that your life is safe in mystery, and that Spirit holds you in the unseen.

Day 1: Entering the Sacred Void

The Elemental Pattern:

The Dark Moon is the womb of becoming. Spirit moves in silence, in unseen ways, in the spaces we often resist. Entering the void isn't about doing—it's about trusting what is forming in the dark.

The Sacred Shift:

Your worth does not depend on constant movement. The pause is holy. The emptiness is not empty at all—it's the soil where Spirit plants what you're not yet ready to see.

The Ritual Repatterning:

Sit in a dim or dark space for 5 minutes. Whisper: "I am safe in the mystery."

Journal Prompt: What does the void feel like to me—fearful, peaceful, or something else? What might Spirit be growing in this unseen place?

Optional: Hold a small object (stone, seed, shell) as a reminder that life begins hidden.

Day 2: Worth Without Proof

The Elemental Pattern:

Spirit asks for faith, not evidence. The Dark Moon teaches you to believe in your worth even when nothing is visible.

The Sacred Shift:

You are not valuable because of what you produce. You are sacred because you exist. Worthiness is not something you earn—it is what you are.

The Ritual Repatterning:

Stand in front of a mirror or place your hand on your heart. Say: "I am worthy, even here."

Journal Prompt: Where have I been waiting for proof of my worth? What would it feel like to believe it without evidence?

Optional: Create a soft blessing for yourself—just one or two sentences that begin with "May I remember…"

Day 3: Meeting Yourself in the Silence

The Elemental Pattern:

Silence is often misunderstood as emptiness, but in spiritual rhythm, silence is sacred presence. It's where the soul echoes most clearly.

The Sacred Shift:

When you turn inward and quiet the noise, you meet the part of yourself that has never been broken. You find the voice behind the voices—the still, soft knowing that whispers, I am whole.

The Ritual Repatterning:

Sit in silence for 5–10 minutes. No music. Just breathe and be.

Journal Prompt: What came up in the silence? Did any part of me speak?

Optional: Write a letter to your inner self, as if greeting a beloved friend.

Day 4: Releasing the Masks

The Elemental Pattern:

The Dark Moon invites you to peel back the layers—to shed identities that were formed from fear, not truth.

The Sacred Shift:

You are allowed to change. You are allowed to return to who you were before the world told you to be someone else. There is nothing selfish in becoming real.

The Ritual Repatterning:

Write down one mask or false role you're ready to release.

Safely burn or bury the paper while saying: "This is no longer mine to wear."

Journal Prompt: Who am I underneath the roles I perform for others?

Day 5: Trusting the Invisible

The Elemental Pattern:

Spirit moves in unseen ways. The Dark Moon is when nothing looks certain—and yet, deep transformation is underway.

The Sacred Shift:

Can you trust even when you don't see it yet? Can you let the mystery hold you, knowing that the seed breaks in darkness long before it blooms in light?

The Ritual Repatterning:

Sit in the dark with a single candle lit. Say: "Even in the void, I am not alone."

Journal Prompt: What would it look like to trust the process without needing proof?

Optional: Write down one area where you choose to surrender control.

Day 6: The Holy Return

The Elemental Pattern:

You've shed, stilled, surrendered. Now you begin to return—gently, slowly, with reverence.

The Sacred Shift:

Your worthiness isn't something you find—it's something you remember. Returning to yourself is an act of holiness.

The Ritual Repatterning:

Write a blessing to your past self: one who forgot, who feared, who tried so hard.

Journal Prompt: What parts of me am I reclaiming as holy?

Light a candle and say: "I return to myself, and I am whole."

Day 7: Walking in Worth

The Elemental Pattern:

Now begins the integration. You carry sacred worth with you—not as a concept, but as a lived truth.

The Sacred Shift:

This journey is not about becoming someone else — it's about remembering the luminous soul you already are. You walk forward now, not because you've proven enough—but because you are enough.

The Ritual Repatterning:

Take a quiet walk or sit in nature. Feel the ground beneath your feet.

Journal Prompt: How has my relationship with worthiness shifted this week?

Optional: Speak a simple vow to yourself: "I walk forward as one who knows her worth."

MY NOTES

WEEK 6: EMOTIONAL PRESENCE & SACRED EXPRESSION

*"You do not have to be fearless to be brave.
You only have to stay." — Unknown.*

Water is the element of flow, of depth, of honesty.
Under the Full Moon, emotions rise like tides. For
many of us, the instinct is to suppress, to control,
to shut down. But your emotions are not here to
drown you. They are here to move you.

The practice of presence is not about solving every
feeling —it is about staying with yourself long enough
to hear what your emotions have to say. Fear, grief, anger,
joy — all of them carry wisdom.

None of them is are mistakes.

This week, you are invited to allow the tides to move. To
trust that presence is enough. To remember that strength
is not the absence of feeling, but the courage to stay present
to it.

May this week bring you gentleness with your own heart,
and may your emotions become rivers that guide you back
to yourself.

Day 1: Allowing the Tide

The Elemental Pattern:

Water teaches movement—waves rise, fall, return. Your emotions are tides, not traps. When you allow them to move, they cleanse rather than consume.

The Sacred Shift:

You don't have to control or fix every feeling. Presence is enough. You are not weak for feeling—you are wise for staying with yourself when the tide comes.

The Ritual Repatterning:

Sit quietly and place your hand over your heart. Whisper: "I allow what comes. I trust what flows."

Journal Prompt: What emotion have I been trying to push away? What happens if I simply let it rise and fall?

Optional: Visualize your feelings as ocean waves, watching them move without trying to stop them.

Day 2: Softening the Shoreline

The Elemental Pattern:

Harsh self-judgment is like a rocky shore—it batters every wave.
Water softens over time when met with gentleness.

The Sacred Shift:

Your emotions don't need fixing—they need a softer landing.
Meeting yourself with compassion changes the way you
experience what you feel.

The Ritual Repatterning:

Hold your face or your heart gently with both hands and say: "I
deserve kindness, even when I hurt."

Journal Prompt: Where am I hardest on myself emotionally?
How can I soften there?

Optional: Place a bowl of water nearby and dip your fingers in as
you write, symbolizing a gentle blessing for your own heart.

Day 3: Sacred Waters of Compassion

The Elemental Pattern:

Water teaches tenderness. When you treat yourself like something fragile and holy, healing begins. Emotional presence doesn't mean drowning in feelings — it means learning how to swim.

The Sacred Shift:

You are not broken for feeling deeply. Sensitivity is not weakness. It's your sacred access point to intuition, to empathy, to Spirit. Compassion begins not just in how you treat others—but how you hold yourself.

The Ritual Repatterning:

Gently place your palm on your cheek or heart and say: "I'm allowed to feel. I'm allowed to be kind to myself."

Journal Prompt: What is one thing I need to forgive myself for feeling?

Optional: Light a candle or float flower petals in a bowl of water as a soft self-honoring ritual.

Day 4: The Wisdom Beneath the Waves

The Elemental Pattern:

Stillness lets the silt settle. When emotions churn, it's hard to see clearly. But beneath the storm, your soul holds ancient knowing.

The Sacred Shift:

Emotions are messengers, not masters. They speak, but they do not define you. Beneath every feeling is a truth. Beneath every truth, a deeper self asking to be known.

The Ritual Repatterning:

Sit in stillness or quiet music. Breathe deeply.

Journal Prompt: What emotion has been loud lately? What might be underneath it?

Bonus: Imagine diving beneath a wave in your mind's eye. What do you find beneath it?

Day 5: Channeling the Flow

The Elemental Pattern:

Water moves, even when it's blocked. If it cannot flow outward, it turns inward. Expression is how we release pressure and restore balance.

The Sacred Shift:

You don't need to be poetic or perfect. Your voice is the valve. Expression is healing—not performance. You were not meant to carry everything inside.

The Ritual Repatterning:

Write a stream-of-consciousness journal entry without editing or filtering.

Speak aloud a feeling you're carrying, even just to yourself.

Optional: Paint, sing, cry, or dance it out. Let something move through you.

Day 6: Emotional Boundaries Are Love

The Elemental Pattern:

Water with no boundary floods everything. Water with a sacred container becomes a healing spring.

The Sacred Shift:

You're allowed to feel everything—and still say "this is mine, that is not." Boundaries don't block love; they clarify it. Emotional maturity is not numbness—it's conscious containment.

The Ritual Repatterning:

Visualize a glowing, gently shifting aura around you—like a watery shield.

Journal Prompt: Where do I take on emotions that don't belong to me? Where do I need firmer boundaries?

Affirm: "I feel deeply. I protect wisely."

Day 7: The Blessing of the Waters

The Elemental Pattern:

At the end of every flood, there's renewal. At the end of
every tear, there's space. Water clears, heals, and blesses.

The Sacred Shift:

Your emotions are sacred rivers. They don't make you too much
— they make you whole. This week has softened
your edges, and within that softening, something new is
growing.

The Ritual Repatterning:

Create a personal water blessing: hold a cup of water,
speak kindness into it, and anoint yourself or sip it gently.

Journal Prompt: How did my relationship to emotion shift this
week?

Optional: Go to water—a shower, bath, stream, or even
visual meditation—and let it hold you.

MY NOTES

WEEK 7: EMPOWERED BECOMING

"Your playing small does not serve the world."
— Marianne Williamson

Fire in the waxing moon grows bold, visible, undeniable.
It is the energy of movement, momentum, and courage.
Yet sometimes what frightens us most is not failure, but
success. Rising means visibility. Becoming means change.
And change often means loss.

It is tempting to play small so others remain comfortable.
To dim so no one feels left behind. But you were not made
to abandon yourself for the sake of others.

Fire reminds you: growth is not betrayal. Success is not selfish.
Your becoming is a gift.

This week, you are invited to face the fear of your own light. To
remember that shining does not steal from others — it
simply illuminates the path. To allow yourself to rise
without apology.

May this week remind you that it is safe to grow, sacred to
succeed, and holy to stand in your own light.

Day 1: The Fear No One Talks About

The Elemental Pattern:

Fire grows in the waxing moon. This is the phase of bold steps and visible momentum. But what if what scares you most isn't failure — it's your power?

The Sacred Shift:

Fear of success is often rooted in fear of change, exposure, responsibility, and loss. But your sacred path doesn't demand perfection—it asks for presence. You can grow without guilt.

The Ritual Repatterning:

Affirm: "It is safe for me to rise."

Journal Prompt: What am I afraid might happen if I succeed?

Light a candle and imagine your future self welcoming you forward.

Day 2: The Sacred Risk of Being Seen

The Elemental Pattern:

Fire needs space to grow. That space is created when you allow yourself to be seen. Visibility is not ego—it's offering.

The Sacred Shift:

When you shrink, others lose the gift of witnessing you bloom. Your soul didn't come here to stay hidden.

The Ritual Repatterning:

Affirm: "My visibility is a gift."

Journal Prompt: Where do I still hide to avoid discomfort?

Share something meaningful with someone safe—or with yourself, in a mirror.

Day 3: Old Stories, New Flame

The Elemental Pattern:

The fire of growth exposes stories you once needed to survive — but that now hold you back.

The Sacred Shift:

It's not your fault you learned to fear joy or attention. But you get to choose what stays. You are not your survival script.

The Ritual Repatterning:

Journal Prompt: What "success story" have I inherited that I don't want?

Light a candle and speak a new truth aloud. Ex: "My success nurtures, not depletes."

Optional: Write your new definition of success.

Day 4: Becoming Requires Burning

The Elemental Pattern:

Waxing fire burns away resistance. This isn't punishment, it's preparation. Becoming often requires letting go.

The Sacred Shift:

To say yes to your next level, you must say goodbye to versions of you that no longer fit. This is a sacred loss. This is a soul upgrade.

The Ritual Repatterning:

Write down a version of you that no longer serves, and burn or release it with intention.

Journal Prompt: What part of me is afraid to be left behind? Can I bless it?

Close with: "I bless my past. I release with love. I rise."

Day 5: The Sacred Yes

The Elemental Pattern:

Fire + Waxing Moon = cosmic momentum. Saying yes today carries long-range power.

The Sacred Shift:

This, yes, is not about hustle or proving. It's about aligned expansion. When you say yes to who you're becoming, your soul stretches into more of itself.

The Ritual Repatterning:

Whisper: "I say yes to my becoming."

Journal Prompt: What am I saying yes to, even if it scares me?

Optional: Step outside and say your yes under the sky.

Day 6: Fire + Embodiment

The Elemental Pattern:

This fire is not just spiritual — it's physical. Your body carries the story of your resistance and your readiness.

The Sacred Shift:

Movement grounds the shift. When you move with intention, you imprint your yes into your cells.

The Ritual Repatterning:

Boldly move your body today: dance, stretch, walk, or shake.

Journal Prompt: Where in my body do I hold fear of being "too much"? What wants to move?

End with this breath: Inhale: I step into myself. Exhale: I am enough.

Day 7: Firelight Reflection

The Elemental Pattern:

Waxing fire invites one final tending before the full illumination. This is the pause before full light.

The Sacred Shift:

You don't need to rush the bloom. Reflection seals the flame into your inner altar. There is nothing that says you have to be the whole flame just yet.

The Ritual Repatterning:

Light a candle and reflect on your journey this week.

Journal Prompt: What surprised me about my relationship with success? What truth do I now carry?

Write a short blessing to your fire

MY NOTES

WEEK 8: SACRED REST + RECIPROCITY

*"You can't pour from an empty cup, but you can fill
oceans when you're whole." — Unknown.*

Air stirs what has grown stagnant. It reveals imbalance and
invites clarity. Under the waning moon, Air shows where
energy has been leaking, where over-giving has left you
depleted, where you have been praised for self-sacrifice at
the expense of your wholeness.

Over-giving is not generosity. It is a forgetting of self. True
reciprocity is the sacred rhythm of giving and receiving — a
breath that flows in and out. Without both, the spirit collapses.

This week, you are invited to name the places where you
have given beyond your capacity. To practice rest as devotion. To
reclaim balance by honoring your needs as much as you
honor others'.

May this week remind you that rest is holy, that your needs are
not a burden, and that you are sacred enough to receive as much
as you give.

Day 1: Naming the Overgiving

The Elemental Pattern:

Air reveals imbalance—it stirs where energy has grown stagnant or depleted. Overgiving happens quietly, almost invisibly, until exhaustion becomes the loudest voice in the room.

The Sacred Shift:

The first act of healing is honesty. Naming where you've overgiven is not selfish — it's sacred clarity.

The Ritual Repatterning:

Whisper aloud: "I see where I've been giving beyond my capacity."

Journal Prompt: Where am I giving from emptiness instead of overflow? Who or what feels heavy rather than holy right now?

Optional: Draw or write a simple symbol for "enough" on your wrist or paper as a reminder today.

Day 2: Breathing Space for Yourself

The Elemental Pattern:

Air expands only when there's space. Your soul needs the same—room to breathe, to rest, to restore.

The Sacred Shift:

Sacred rest is not laziness—it is reciprocity with yourself. Every exhale needs an inhale. One of the greatest shifts you will ever make is learning that your being is not proven by your doing. It is a quiet rebellion, and a necessary return.

The Ritual Repatterning:

Take three intentional breaths. With each inhale, whisper: "I receive." With each exhale: "I release."

Journal Prompt: Where can I create just 10 minutes of space for myself today? What would feel like true rest?

Optional: Open a window or step outside, imagining fresh air filling every depleted place in you.

Day 3: The Sacred Yes to Rest

The Elemental Pattern:

Air teaches that saying yes to what restores you is as important as saying no to what drains you. Rest is not indulgence—it's preparation for the sacred work ahead.

The Sacred Shift:

Every moment you give yourself permission to rest, you remind your soul that you matter too.

The Ritual Repatterning:

Choose one restful act today and commit to it, even if brief—tea, silence, stretching, stillness.

Journal Prompt: What does rest feel like in my body? Where have I been denying it?

Optional: Speak aloud before you rest: "This rest is holy. I receive it fully."

Day 4: Sacred Refusal

The Elemental Pattern:

Air clears by movement—but also by release. Saying no is a way to create oxygen in your life.

The Sacred Shift:

Refusal is not rejection. It's protection. When you honor your no, you protect the sacred energy needed to say yes to what truly matters.

The Ritual Repatterning:

Speak aloud: "I do not owe anyone my exhaustion."

Journal Prompt: Where is a "no" rising in me? What does it need to be honored?

Optional: Write a practice refusal you wish you'd given yourself in the past. You never have to send it—this is for your soul.

Day 5: Receive to Remember

The Elemental Pattern:

Inhale. Pause. Exhale. This is the breath of giving and receiving. You weren't made to exhale only.

The Sacred Shift:

Allowing yourself to receive is an act of spiritual reclamation. You are not a burden. You are worthy of replenishment.

The Ritual Repatterning:

Lay down or sit quietly with hands open, palms facing up. Whisper: "I am open to receive."

Journal Prompt: When was the last time I allowed someone, or something, to support me?

Optional: Let someone help you today. Even something small. Notice how your body responds.

Day 6: Rewriting the Role

The Elemental Pattern:

Air carries stories. Some of the most exhausting roles
we play are inherited ones—caretaker, fixer, martyr,
peacekeeper. Our parents, teachers, friends and lovers
have all contributed in the teaching of a role that we
needed to be in their lives.

The Sacred Shift:

You are allowed to rewrite the role you play in your life. You
do not have to keep performing an identity that depletes you.

The Ritual Repatterning:

Write down the role you were taught to play.

Journal Prompt: If I could create a new role that honors
my truth and energy, what would it be called? How would
it feel?

Optional: Tear or burn the old role with intention: "I release this
story."

Day 7: Sacred Reciprocity

The Elemental Pattern:

Air flows in all directions. True balance is found not in isolation but in sacred mutuality.

The Sacred Shift:

You are part of an ecosystem of giving and receiving. When you let yourself rest, you re-enter that system in wholeness not depletion.

The Ritual Repatterning:

Reflect: Who gives to you without expectation? How do you give in return?

Journal Prompt: What does sacred reciprocity feel like in my body and relationships?

Optional: Write or speak a blessing for your future: "I give and receive in sacred balance. I am not alone in the giving."

MY NOTES

WEEK 9: COMPARISON → INNER TRUTH + UNIQUE LIGHT

"A flower does not think of competing with the flower next to it. It just blooms." — Zen Shin.

Air carries voices — loud, endless, competing. Under the Full Moon, comparison grows sharp as we measure ourselves against others' paths, bodies, gifts, or timing. But a flower does not bloom by competing with another. It blooms by staying rooted in its own soil.

Comparison distracts us from our soul's path. It convinces us we are behind when in truth we are right on time. Your journey was never meant to look like anyone else's. Your light was never meant to match another's flame.

This week, you are invited to return to your own breath. To notice when you drift into others' winds and gently come back to yourself. To trust that your life is unfolding in its own rhythm, in its own beauty.

May this week bring you home to the truth of your unique light, reminding you that your becoming is exactly on time.

Day 1: Noticing the Drift

The Elemental Pattern:

Air carries many voices. Some encouraging, some distracting.
Comparison is what happens when you drift too far into
other people's winds, forgetting your own breath.

The Sacred Shift:

You cannot hear your soul clearly while listening to everyone
else's. Today, you gently notice where you've drifted, not with
judgment, but with compassion.

The Ritual Repatterning:

Whisper: "I return to my own breath."

Journal Prompt: Where have I been caught in comparison lately?
Whose path have I been measuring mine against?

Optional: Close your eyes and visualize gently turning back
toward your own inner current.

Day 2: The Truth Beneath Envy

The Elemental Pattern:

Envy, like wind, points toward movement—it shows you what you secretly long for. Beneath every pang of comparison is a hidden desire waiting to be honored.

The Sacred Shift:

Instead of shame, meet your envy with curiosity. It may be pointing you back to something your soul deeply wants to grow.

The Ritual Repatterning:

Whisper: "Every longing shows me who I am becoming."

Journal Prompt: Who or what have I felt envious of lately? What does that envy reveal about what I deeply desire?

Optional: Write a single action step to honor that desire in a way that's uniquely yours.

Day 3: Clearing the Air of Judgment

The Elemental Pattern:

Comparison thrives in stale air—spaces full of unspoken judgments and rigid expectations. Air wants to move freely, clearing old patterns of "should" and "better than."

The Sacred Shift:

You are allowed to open the windows of your soul, letting in fresh truth. You are not meant to live in someone else's sky.

The Ritual Repatterning:

Open a window or stand outside. Whisper: "I release what is not mine to carry."

Journal Prompt: What judgments (of myself or others) am I ready to let go of?

Optional: On a piece of paper, write one comparison thought and tear it up as you breathe deeply.

Day 4: The Breath of Belonging

The Elemental Pattern:

Air connects everything, yet each current is unique.
Belonging doesn't mean blending in—it means
honoring your own breath while respecting the whole.

The Sacred Shift:

You don't have to shrink to belong. Your unique light
contributes to the greater harmony.

The Ritual Repatterning:

Sit quietly and place a hand on your chest. Feel your chest move,
and as you do, whisper: "I belong as I am."

Journal Prompt: Where do I feel most like myself? How can I
honor that space more fully?

Optional: Light a candle or incense as a symbol of your light
adding to the collective.

Day 5: Claiming Your Light

The Elemental Pattern:

Air holds the spectrum—from storm to breeze, from whisper to shout. You do not need to shout to be powerful. Your light carries on your breath, not your volume.

The Sacred Shift:

You do not need to be anyone else to be radiant. You are luminous in your truth. Comparison dims; authenticity shines.

The Ritual Repatterning:

Close your eyes and place your hand on your chest. Whisper: "I claim my light."

Journal Prompt: Where have I been trying to mimic someone else's light? What is mine alone?

Optional: Light a candle as a symbol of your truth.

Day 6: Inner Compass

The Elemental Pattern:

Air may carry you far, but it's your soul that chooses the direction. Stillness lets your inner compass realign.

The Sacred Shift:

Even amidst noise, you can tune inward. When you stop scanning the world for answers, you find that your own soul has been whispering all along.

The Ritual Repatterning:

Sit in silence for 5–10 minutes with your eyes closed. Focus on your breath.

Journal Prompt: What has my inner compass been trying to tell me lately? Where is it pointing?

Optional: Create a simple symbol (sigil or drawing) to represent this direction.

Day 7: The Blessing of the Breath

The Elemental Pattern:

Breath is your first connection to this world—and your constant companion. When the world overwhelms, the breath remains.

The Sacred Shift:

Your life is already a prayer in motion. Your breath is sacred. Let it return you to the quiet miracle of being you.

The Ritual Repatterning:

Do a gentle breath meditation: Inhale through the nose, exhale through the mouth for 5 minutes.

Journal Prompt: What truth do I want to carry forward with me from this week?

MY NOTES

WEEK 10: DOUBT → DIVINE CONNECTION + FAITH

"Faith is the bird that feels the light and sings when the dawn is still dark." — Rabindranath Tagore.

The First Quarter Moon is a time of tension — the stretch between beginning and breakthrough. Spirit meets us here, in the place where doubt grows loud. Doubt often masquerades as logic, as caution, as protection.

But beneath it lies an ache: the fear that Spirit will not catch us when we leap.

Faith is not the absence of questions. It is the courage to trust anyway. Spirit does not demand fearlessness. It simply asks us to listen beneath the noise, to the quiet voice that never leaves.

This week, you are invited to meet doubt with gentleness. To ask what it is protecting, and then to choose trust anyway. To let faith grow not despite your questions, but through them.

May this week restore your confidence that you are not alone, that you are guided, and that Spirit has always been holding you — even here.

Day 1: The Voice That Shakes

The Elemental Pattern:

Doubt can sound like wisdom. It mimics logic, echoes caution, and pretends to protect. But underneath it often lies an old ache — the fear that Spirit will not catch you when you leap.

The Sacred Shift:

Your fear is not foolish — it's a relic of when you felt alone. But you are not alone anymore. Spirit has never needed you to be fearless. It only ever asked you to listen beneath the noise.

The Ritual Repatterning:

Light a candle and place your hand on your throat. Speak: "I trust the voice beneath the doubt."

Journal Prompt: What does my doubt try to protect me from? What if I didn't need protecting anymore?

Optional: Brew a cup of calming tea (e.g., chamomile, lemon balm) and listen to your breath as you sip it slowly.

Day 2: Spirit Knows Before You Do

The Elemental Pattern:

Spirit doesn't demand certainty—it invites trust. And trust
is often built not in lightning bolts of revelation, but in
slow, quiet echoes. You may not know where you're going,
but Spirit already walks there.

The Sacred Shift:

You do not need to understand to be guided. The map is
encoded in your spirit. Faith is not about erasing doubt;
it's about believing that something greater still holds
you in the dark.

The Ritual Repatterning:

Whisper aloud: "I am already being led, even here."

Journal Prompt: Where in my life do I sense I'm being
guided, even if I don't see the way?

Optional practice: Hold a small item (stone, shell, leaf) and ask it
to remind you that Spirit leads even in stillness.
Carry it today.

Day 3: Tuning In

The Elemental Pattern:

Faith is a frequency. It is not a rigid belief—it is a soft presence that you tune into. Doubt will always offer its static. Your task is to return to the stillness beneath it.

The Sacred Shift:

Spirit isn't hiding. It's whispering. When you slow down enough to listen—not to your fear, but to your soul— you'll find you've always known.

The Ritual Repatterning:

Sit in silence for five minutes. Breathe deeply.
Say: "I tune in to what is true."

Journal Prompt: When did I last feel connected to something greater? What did it feel like in my body?

Optional: Write a short prayer, poem, or letter to Spirit from your heart.

Day 4: The Companion of Doubt

The Elemental Pattern:

What if doubt isn't your enemy? What if it's a part of you asking for reassurance, not rejection?

The Sacred Shift:

You don't have to exile your doubt to have faith. You can bring it along. Let it witness the sacred anyway. Even when it questions, you can keep walking.

The Ritual Repatterning:

Light a candle and name your doubt. Say, "You may come, but you will not lead."

Journal Prompt: What is my doubt really asking me for? What reassurance does it need?

Optional: Write a letter from your Higher Self to your doubt.

Day 5: Signs and Synchronicities

The Elemental Pattern:

Faith often returns through the door of wonder. Spirit speaks in signs, not always grand, but always timely.

The Sacred Shift:

The more you notice, the more you're shown. Not because the signs weren't there, but because now you're ready to see.

The Ritual Repatterning:

Set an intention to notice a sign today. Ask for one gently, then let go.

Journal Prompt: What signs or synchronicities have shown up in my life before? Did I believe them?

Optional: Create a small altar or space with 1–3 sacred objects that remind you of connection.

Day 6: Sacred Evidence

The Elemental Pattern:

Sometimes, faith is just remembering. Not imagining, or hoping, but returning to the evidence that you were never forsaken.

The Sacred Shift:

The moment you think you've never been held is the moment to recall the time you were. Faith isn't blind; it's deeply rooted in what you've already survived.

The Ritual Repatterning:

Write a list of 5 times Spirit showed up for you (directly or subtly).

Journal Prompt: How can I anchor these memories when doubt visits again?

Optional: Speak aloud: "I carry proof in my bones."

Day 7: The Return to Knowing

The Elemental Pattern:

Doubt will always exist. But it doesn't have to lead.
Faith is not a feeling; it is a choice you return to, again
and again.

The Sacred Shift:

You are not behind. You are on your way. The fact that
you're still asking, still opening, still returning, that's
your proof. Spirit has never stopped walking with you,
even when you questioned the way.

The Ritual Repatterning:

Light a candle for your path. Say aloud: "I return to trust."

Journal Prompt: What does faith feel like in me now, after
this week? What old doubts feel softer or quieter?

Optional: Create a short night prayer or mantra to repeat
before bed this week, such as: "Even in the dark, I am guided."

MY NOTES

WEEK 11: IMPATIENCE →
SACRED TIMING

*"Adopt the pace of nature: her secret is
patience." — Ralph Waldo Emerson.*

The Gibbous Moon swells with promise, almost full,
almost ready. Impatience rises here, whispering that you
are behind, that you must rush, that if you do not hurry,
you will miss your chance. But impatience is not truth,
it is fear in disguise.

Spirit teaches that what is yours cannot pass you by. The soul
does not bloom late. Sacred timing is not about speed; it is about
alignment. When the moment is ripe, it will open naturally.

This week, you are invited to release the false clock. To trust that
you are unfolding in divine rhythm. To breathe into the waiting
and discover its wisdom.

May this week remind you that you are not behind, that your
pace is holy, and that the timing of your soul is always right on
time.

Day 1: The Energy of Impatience

The Elemental Pattern:

Impatience is often disguised as urgency, but it's really a sign that our spirit feels unsafe. When the soul is trusting, it flows. When the soul is afraid, it rushes.

The Sacred Shift:

What if you are not late? What if your life is unfolding in divine sequence, even in its delays? There is a reason for the timing of your shift. What could be trying to keep you from moving forward?

The Ritual Repatterning:

Sit with your breath and say: "I am right on time."

Journal Prompt: Where in my life do I feel behind? Whose timeline am I trying to live by?

Day 2: Slowing to Hear Spirit

The Elemental Pattern:

The gibbous moon rises almost full, but not yet. It teaches the power of the almost. Of the pause before culmination.

The Sacred Shift:

Just like the semi-colon in a sentence, it is that pause, Spirit often whispers. The deeper guidance isn't loud—it waits for your presence, not your performance. There is more that is waiting for you.

The Ritual Repatterning:

Take 3 minutes in silence. No music, no agenda. Just listen.

Journal Prompt: What would it mean to believe I don't have to hurry?

Day 3: Unlearning Urgency

The Elemental Pattern:

You were taught that quickness equals value. It became a race, that somehow was going to create more acceptance. But soul work is slow. It spirals. It revisits. It roots.

The Sacred Shift:

To repattern, we must bless the slow bloom. A bulb is planted in the ground resting during winter, and starts growing before it blooms in spring and summer. We don't see the shoots before they become the plant that brings beauty into our lives. The same is true of the soul.

The Ritual Repatterning:

Light a candle and say: "I honor the pace of my soul."

Journal Prompt: What has grown slowly in my life but meaningfully?

Day 4: Sacred Timing Is Not Passive

The Elemental Pattern:

Trusting timing isn't the same as doing nothing. It means aligned action—not frantic reaction.

The Sacred Shift:

Your energy moves best when it's rooted in resonance, not reaction. Sacred timing is not rushed. It speaks through resonance, and your body carries the dictionary. There will be moments you recognize without explanation, because your body speaks in a language older than thought. You are remembering its dictionary.

The Ritual Repatterning:

Ask your body: What is mine to act on today? What is not?

Journal Prompt: What happens when I wait for clarity before acting?

Day 5: The Almost Phase

The Elemental Pattern:

Impatience spikes when we're near a breakthrough. That's when ego gets loud and faith is tested.

The Sacred Shift:

Impatience is not failure, it is the restless glow of ripening, the way the gibbous moon swells just before it shines full. If we wait just a little longer, the shine will be brighter than the dark.

The Ritual Repatterning:

Place your hand on your heart and say: "I will not sabotage what is still becoming."

Journal Prompt: What old story makes me want to quit too soon?

Day 6: Miracles Are Not Always Immediate

The Elemental Pattern:

We forget: nature creates slowly. Spirit manifests in rhythm, not in rush.

The Sacred Shift:

Every shift you've made has laid groundwork. Trust what you can't yet see.

The Ritual Repatterning:

Write down one thing you've been waiting on

.

Bless it: "I trust your timing."

Journal Prompt: Where is Spirit asking me to hold faith in the unseen?

Day 7: Sacred Timing Is Soul Trust

The Elemental Pattern:

Impatience weakens when trust grows. Today, let yourself feel what it's like to be carried by something wiser.

The Sacred Shift:

You are not behind. You are being led. You are not late, you are blooming at the speed of your soul.

The Ritual Repatterning:

Spend 5 minutes outside or by a window, observing nature's pace.

Journal Prompt: What has this week taught me about how Spirit moves in me?

MY NOTES

WEEK 12: SELF-SABOTAGE →
DEVOTED ALIGNMENT

"You are allowed to start again, as many times as it takes." — Unknown.

Self-sabotage often appears right before success. It whispers delays, distractions, and excuses. It looks like laziness, but beneath it lies fear — fear of exposure, of joy, of change. The waning moon in Fire asks us to see these patterns clearly and to choose devotion instead.

You do not need harsher discipline to break the cycle. You need deeper love. Devotion is what steadies the flame when fear tries to blow it out. Alignment is what keeps you walking forward when the old patterns beg you to retreat.

This week, you are invited to meet your sabotage with compassion. To thank it for trying to protect you, and then to choose a new way. To practice devotion not as punishment, but as a sacred agreement with your own becoming.

May this week teach you to walk in alignment with your truth, and to keep your flame steady, even through fear.

Day 1: Seeing the Pattern

The Elemental Pattern:

Self-sabotage is often quiet. It hides in delays, excuses, and the small ways you pull away right when things begin to bloom. Spirit invites you to see it now, not with shame, but with love.

The Sacred Shift:

You cannot heal what you refuse to see. Seeing your pattern clearly is not failure—it's the first step toward freedom.

The Ritual Repatterning:

Whisper: "I see where I hold myself back, and I choose differently now."

Journal Prompt: What patterns show up right before I sabotage myself? What fear are they trying to protect me from?

Optional: Place your hand on your heart and say:
"Thank you for trying to protect me. I choose a new way."

Day 2: Forgiving the False Starts

The Elemental Pattern:

Every time you stopped, delayed, or quit, it was never because you were broken; it was because you were afraid. Forgiving yourself softens the edges of shame, making room for devotion.

The Sacred Shift:

You do not need to punish yourself for the past. Forgiveness clears the way for consistent alignment because love, not fear, builds lasting change.

The Ritual Repatterning:

Light a candle and whisper: "I forgive every false start. I begin again."

Journal Prompt: What would change if I believed my past attempts were practice, not failure?

Optional: Write a gentle letter to the "past you" who tried and stopped. End with: "I love you for trying."

Day 3: The Habit of Almost

The Elemental Pattern:

You've gotten close before—so close. But something in you pulls away at the edge of arrival. You sabotage not because you don't want it, but because it asks you to become someone new.

The Sacred Shift:

Almost is a ghost you no longer have to dance with. You are not too late. You are not behind. You are just becoming brave enough to stay when things start to work.

The Ritual Repatterning:

Say: "I choose completion over chaos."

Journal Prompt: What stories do I tell myself right before I quit or pull back?

Optional: Revisit one unfinished thing and complete a single step.

Day 4: The Lie of "I'll Start Over Monday"

The Elemental Pattern:

How many times have you delayed your becoming because of a calendar? The lie says: Later will be better. The truth is: Your life is now.

The Sacred Shift:

Devoted alignment begins in this breath—not in a perfect Monday. Not in next month's plan. Not when you lose weight or prove yourself or get it all together.

The Ritual Repatterning:

Breathe in this truth: "I begin again in this moment."

Journal Prompt: What is my spirit really asking me to begin again today?

Optional: Do one nourishing thing now, however small.

Day 5: Micro-Alignments Matter

The Elemental Pattern:

Not everything sacred is grand. Some of the most powerful acts of devotion are invisible—choosing water over wine, rest over scrolling, silence over proving.

The Sacred Shift:

Self-sabotage ends when you realize you don't have to move mountains—you just have to keep walking. One aligned step at a time builds a path.

The Ritual Repatterning:

Whisper: "My small steps are sacred."

Journal Prompt: What is one micro-alignment I can choose today?

Optional: Track 3 small choices throughout the day and honor each.

Day 6: Trusting Yourself Again

The Elemental Pattern:

After enough sabotage, you stop believing in yourself. Promises begin to feel hollow. But trust isn't built in declarations—it's rebuilt in consistency.

The Sacred Shift:

Forgive the false starts. The breaking of oaths. You were learning. Begin again not with a vow—but with a touch of grace and a single step.

The Ritual Repatterning:

Light a candle and say: "I am worthy of my own trust."

Journal Prompt: What does self-trust mean to me today? What would rebuild it?

Optional: Pour a glass of water and drink it with intention as a ritual of renewal.

Day 7: Sacred Recommitment

The Elemental Pattern:

Devotion is not about being perfect. It's about coming home again and again. It's about remembering what matters even when it's hard.

The Sacred Shift:

This is your sacred rhythm now—not a sprint, not a cycle of sabotage, but a soul-deep remembering. Recommit not to an outcome, but to the way you want to walk.

The Ritual Repatterning:

Create a personal recommitment mantra. (e.g., "I walk with grace. I rise with love. I stay with Spirit.")

Journal Prompt: What does devotion mean to me now, after this week?

Optional: Write a letter to your future self—a soul reminder to come back to alignment when you forget.

MY NOTES

WEEK 13: RESISTANCE →
REBIRTH + INTEGRATION

"The butterfly is proof that resistance is part
of transformation." — Unknown.

At the edge of transformation, resistance always rises.
It says: you cannot change. You should turn back. Nothing will
be different.

But resistance is not proof of failure — it is proof that you
are close.

The Full Moon in Spirit illuminates this truth: resistance is
the final gate before rebirth. It is the trembling of the soul
just before it expands. To meet resistance is to know you
are on holy ground.

This week, you are invited to meet resistance with curiosity. To
ask what it is protecting. To listen for the fear beneath it, and
then to step forward anyway. Integration is not easy,
but it is sacred.

May this week carry you through the gate of resistance, into the
fullness of rebirth, and into the holy integration of all
you have become.

Day 1: Meeting Resistance
with Curiosity

The Elemental Pattern:

Resistance is the soul's way of saying: Something important is happening here. It's not proof you're failing—it's proof you're close to change.

The Sacred Shift:

Instead of fighting your resistance, ask it why it's here. Often, it's protecting an old version of you that doesn't know you're safe now.

The Ritual Repatterning:

Whisper: "Resistance, I see you. What are you trying to protect?"

Journal Prompt: What am I resisting right now? What fear lives underneath it?

Optional: Place your hand on your heart and say: "Thank you for trying to protect me. I choose to grow anyway."

Day 2: Honoring the Old Self

The Elemental Pattern:

Before rebirth comes a soft goodbye. The self you've carried you
this far. You honor it, not with shame, but with gratitude.

The Sacred Shift:

You don't have to hate who you were to become who you
are. Letting go is love, not rejection. You had to be that
person then to be the person you are becoming.

The Ritual Repatterning:

Light a candle for the version of you that is fading.
Whisper: "I honor you. You brought me here."

Journal Prompt: What gifts did my old self give me? What
am I ready to release as I step forward?

Optional: Write the words: "Thank you. I release you with love,"
and keep or burn it as a ritual of closure.

Day 3: The Sacred Pause

The Elemental Pattern:

After the storm of resistance, stillness can feel unfamiliar. But Spirit teaches that rest is not the end—it is the womb of rebirth.

The Sacred Shift:

Integration requires rest. A sacred pause isn't quitting—it's allowing your energy to recalibrate so you can receive what is truly yours.

The Ritual Repatterning:

Light a candle and sit in silence for 5–10 minutes. Let your breath be your only guide.

Journal Prompt: What is coming alive in the quiet? What fears try to fill the silence?

Affirm: "I am allowed to rest. I trust what is becoming in me."

Day 4: Rebirth is Not a Performance

The Elemental Pattern:

We're taught that transformation should look dramatic, like phoenix fire or epic change. But often, it's subtle, soft, and invisible to the outside world.

The Sacred Shift:

You don't have to prove your healing. You don't have to explain your rebirth. Becoming is internal first, then embodied. Trust your process.

The Ritual Repatterning:

Journal Prompt: Where have I felt pressure to "show" my growth? What does true becoming feel like instead?

Optional: Create a quiet symbol of your rebirth—a drawing, color, word, or object.

Speak: "I honor the becoming I don't need to explain."

Day 5: Walking Between Worlds

The Elemental Pattern:

This week bridges everything—the old and the new, the seen and unseen, the sacred and shadowed. You are walking between them now.

The Sacred Shift:

You've become the bridge. Your story now holds medicine—not because it was perfect, but because you lived it with courage.

The Ritual Repatterning:

Light two candles (one for who you were, one for who you are becoming). Sit between them.

Journal Prompt: What wisdom lives in the in-between?

Blessing: "I walk forward whole. Nothing was wasted. All of me belongs."

Day 6: Integration as Devotion

The Elemental Pattern:

Spirit reminds us that daily life is a temple. Integration isn't a single moment — it's returning again and again to who you truly are.

The Sacred Shift:

Your practices, pauses, and prayers are how you integrate. Let devotion become your new rhythm—not perfection, but presence.

The Ritual Repatterning:

Reflect on one ritual from this journey you want to keep. Begin weaving it into your day.

Journal Prompt: What does a life of sacred integration look like for me?

Affirm: "My life is my altar. I return to myself with love."

Day 7: The Soft Resurrection

The Elemental Pattern:

Not all rebirths arrive with lightning. Some come gently, through breath, through grace, through the quiet choice to keep going.

The Sacred Shift:

You are not the same—and that is sacred. Celebrate softly, breathe deeply, and bless the path that brought you here.

The Ritual Repatterning:

Create a small offering to yourself (a flower, poem, cup of tea, moment of stillness).

Journal Prompt: Who am I now? What am I carrying forward—and what am I laying down?

Speak: "This is my resurrection. I rise in wholeness."

MY NOTES

REFLECTIONS —

"The wound is the place where the Light enters you." – Rumi

As we complete this 90-day journey of Sacred Repatterning,
you stand at the threshold of integration.

The elements have moved through you. The moon has mirrored your
cycles. You have burned away old habits, rested in water's
wisdom, built new truths in the earth, spoken clarity through air, and
listened to the call of Spirit.

You return now, a truer version of yourself—rooted, radiant, and
aligned. These patterns are no longer ideas; they are becoming
your breath, your rhythm, your life. You have laid a new foundation,
one rooted in truth and rhythm. You've walked with the elements,
embraced the cycles, and said yes to becoming.

If you feel called, linger here. Walk these weeks again, slowly, as often
as you need. Each return will show you something new,
because you will be new each time you walk it.

And when you are ready, the path to the next rhythm awaits—
where devotion becomes daily breath, and presence becomes
the way you live.

 Now comes the quiet work of presence. The living of the truth you've
claimed.

Final Journal Prompt: What would it mean to live a life of
devoted presence?

MY NOTES

THE BLESSING OF RETURN

Blessed is the one who dares to begin again, who gives thanks not only for light, but for the seasons of undoing.

May the fire of your intention keep you warm.

May the waters of grace flow freely in your life.

May the air of clarity whisper truth to your spirit.

May the earth of your devotion root you in sacred rhythm.

And may Spirit continue to remind you:

You are the pattern, and the prayer.

AFTERWORD

You have walked through the elements, practiced release, and reshaped what no longer serves.

This is the work of *Sacred Repatterning*: honoring the visible rhythms that hold us steady — Fire, Water, Earth, Air, and Spirit. But as one layer of practice closes, another begins.

Beneath the elements lies something quieter: the Hidden Pattern.

These are the currents we do not always see — the habits of thought, the subtle reflexes of fear or hope, the ways we show up in ordinary days without even thinking.

Devoted Presence will ask us to turn toward these hidden patterns, not to judge them, but to soften them in the light of love. It is here that devotion becomes daily, steady, lived. Not only reframed, but practiced.

It invites you into this next step: to discover the hidden patterns shaping your soul, and to transform them into rhythms of presence, mercy, and truth.

ACKNOWLEDGEMENTS

To the broken habits, the unraveling days,
and the sacred pause —
Thank you for showing me that healing lives in rhythm.

To the friends, and soul companions who held
space while I rewove my life —
Your presence allowed me to rest and begin again.

To the elements — fire, earth, air, water, and spirit —
You taught me how to live in harmony with myself.

To every person learning to rebuild from the inside out —
May this book feel like a hand in yours.

Thank you to those who walked with me and to every sacred
soul who chooses to rise with intention—this is for you.

To the weary soul, may these pages be water.
To the searching heart, may these words be light.
To the hidden self, may this space be safe.

You are not broken.

You are becoming.

www.ingramcontent.com/pod-product-compliance
Lightning Source LLC
LaVergne TN
LVHW041225080426
835508LV00011B/1086